Navigating the Legal Maze

Regulations and Compliance in the Blockchain Universe

Table of Contents

Chapter 1. Introduction

Navigating the complex labyrinth of legal boundaries known as blockchain regulations is a feat that demands diligent research and sagacious understanding. Our Special Report on "Navigating the Legal Maze: Regulations and Compliance in the Blockchain Universe" comprehensively breaks down these seemingly convoluted concepts into simple, comprehensible pieces for the average reader. It explores the multifaceted regulatory framework surrounding blockchain technologies and provides guidance for robust compliance practices, all while keeping your interest alive with practical examples and relatable scenarios. Regardless if you are a tech-savvy blockchain enthusiast or a newcomer to the digital frontier, our report expertly maneuvers through the intricate web of legislation and protocols to equip you with the essential tools for a confident stride into the blockchain universe. So why wait? The power to understand and imbibe blockchain regulations can be at your fingertips today!

Chapter 2. Introduction to Blockchain and the Legal Landscape

To lay the foundation for understanding the legal complexities that intertwine with blockchain technology, it is critical to gain a robust conceptual grasp of what this technology encompasses. Hence, we commence this journey of exploration at the intersection of technology and law.

Blockchain, often associated with cryptocurrencies like Bitcoin and Ether, is a type of distributed ledger technology (DLT) designed to keep track of transactions or digital interactions in a decentralized, transparent way, resistant to editing or modification. This technology operates on three core principles - decentralization, immutability, and transparency, each adding a layer of complexity to the regulatory measures that govern their application and use.

2.1. Decentralization

Unlike traditional systems grounded on central authorities like banks or governments to oversee and verify transactions, blockchain is inherently decentralized. This means that no single entity has control over the entire network. Instead, operations are distributed across a network of computers, referred to as nodes, each holding an identical copy of the blockchain. Nodes are responsible for validating and recording new transactions onto the blockchain, a process achieved through consensus mechanisms, contributing to the network's security.

Decentralization eliminates the need for an intermediary, thereby increasing efficiency and reducing costs. However, this very attribute places blockchain in murky regulatory waters. With no central authority to hold accountable, pinpointing liability in cases of illegal activities or disputes becomes complex.

2.2. Immutability

Immutability refers to the unalterable nature of the blockchain. Once a transaction is validated and added to the blockchain, it cannot be changed, reversed, or deleted, providing a level of data integrity and transparency that traditional systems struggle to match. This feature provides a level of certainty and trust in the transactional data the blockchain holds, as it ensures that historical transactions remain intact and auditable.

While immutability enhances data security, it also raises legal concerns. Issues around data privacy, particularly in regard to regulatory standards like the General Data Protection Regulation (GDPR) in Europe, which includes the "right to be forgotten," pose a distinct challenge to the permanent nature of blockchain.

2.3. Transparency

All transactions on the blockchain are transparent and visible to all participants in the network. This transparency significantly reduces the risk of fraudulent activity, as manipulative actions are immediately evident to all network participants.

However, the public visibility of transactions also stirs privacy concerns. Although transactional data are typically pseudonymized, sophisticated network analysis can sometimes uncover the identities behind the transactions, potentially leading to unwanted exposure and enhanced scrutiny from surveillance bodies.

As we navigate through the regulatory landscape of blockchain, remember that these concepts: decentralization, immutability, and transparency shape how and why such regulations exist, and why some of the seemingly clear-cut legal principles encounter stumbling blocks in their application. Grasping this is the first step toward understanding the legal maze surrounding blockchain.

Now, let's delve into the legal environment.

Every technology, including blockchain, doesn't operate in a vacuum. It is subjected to various regulatory jurisdictions, each with its frameworks and interpretations. Alongside these, we have guidelines and recommendations from global institutions like the Financial Action Task Force (FATF), which further influence regional regulations.

Blockchain, used in various applications from finance to supply chain, health, real estate, and even voting, finds itself subjected to a host of potentially applicable regulations. These fall into broad categories: financial and securities regulations, privacy and data protection laws, and other sector-specific regulations.

2.4. Financial and Securities Regulations

These regulations primarily relate to cryptocurrencies, ICOs (Initial Coin Offerings), and other digital assets. Authorities like the U.S Securities and Exchange Commission (SEC), the U.K's Financial Conduct Authority (FCA), and many others have set various rules and guidelines to protect consumers and maintain market integrity. The challenge? Classifying blockchain-based assets (like identifying if they should be treated as a security or as currency), dealing with frauds, market manipulation, and irregularities.

2.5. Privacy and Data Protection Regulations

The global surge of data privacy laws like Europe's GDPR or California's CCPA is shaping blockchain regulations. The very nature of blockchain raises numerous privacy issues. Policymakers across the globe grapple with reconciling these laws with blockchain's inherent characteristics like immutability and pseudonymisation.

2.6. Sector-Specific Regulations

Depending on the application of blockchain, several industry-specific regulations come into play. Blockchain in healthcare dealing with patient data will need to comply with the Health Insurance Portability and Accountability Act (HIPAA) in the U.S. Similarly, supply chain application will need to mind trade laws.

Navigating any technology within the legal dimensions requires careful balancing of the benefits against the risks. In the following chapters, we will delve into how different jurisdictions tackle blockchain regulations, how businesses can design and implement compliance programs, and how regulations might shape up in the future.

Chapter 3. Regulatory Framework: A Global Overview

Establishing an understanding of the global regulatory landscape is the first point of embarkment on our journey to comprehending the labyrinth of blockchain regulations. The regulatory frameworks differ vastly from one nation to another, hence, it is imperative to take a holistic view of the global regulatory landscape surrounding blockchain and its applications.

3.1. The United States: Federal and State-Specific Regulations

The United States presents a complex regulatory landscape due to its multi-layered approach, incorporating both federal and state-specific regulations.

At the federal level, the Securities and Exchange Commission (SEC) focuses on the applicability of securities laws to Initial Coin Offerings (ICOs) and other token sale events. The SEC considers tokens issued during ICOs as securities, thereby bringing them under the purview of federal securities law.

Additionally, the Commodities and Futures Trading Commission (CFTC) treats cryptocurrencies like Bitcoin as commodities, implying that the derivative contracts related to such cryptocurrencies, fall under its jurisdiction. Another federal agency heavily involved in cryptocurrency regulation is the Financial Crimes Enforcement Network (FinCEN), which requires money services businesses to maintain certain Anti-Money Laundering/Countering the Financing of Terrorism (AML/CFT) programs.

On the state level, the specifics of legislation vary significantly. For instance, New York implemented the stringent BitLicense regulations in 2015, which apply to any business engaging in virtual currency activities in the state.

3.2. The European Union: Unified yet Flexible Approach

The European Union (EU), on its part, has taken a more unified yet flexible approach towards blockchain and cryptocurrency regulations. Its primary aim is to facilitate innovation while ensuring financial stability and investor protection.

The European Securities and Markets Authority (ESMA) provided guidance that the existing EU regulations could apply to tokens depending on their classification. Additionally, the Fifth Anti-Money Laundering Directive (5AMLD), implemented in 2020, is the first EU law to directly address cryptocurrency-related AML/CFT.

In an endeavor to standardize regulations, the European Commission presented the Markets in Crypto-assets (MiCA) regulations. MiCA brings all crypto-assets not covered under existing EU financial services legislation into its ambit, providing legal certainty for issuers and service providers.

3.3. Asia: Blend of Tight Controls and Embracing Innovation

The Asian continent presents a blend of tight controls and embracing blockchain innovation.

China, while effectively banning cryptocurrencies, has invested heavily in developing blockchain technology. Its Digital Currency Electronic Payment (DCEP) initiative aims at launching a state-backed digital currency.

In contrast, Japan has embraced crypto-assets, recognizing Bitcoin as a legal method of payment and providing a legal framework for exchange operators.

Singapore takes a balanced approach. The Monetary Authority of Singapore (MAS) focuses on regulating the activities surrounding digital tokens rather than the tokens themselves. The Payment Services Act, introduced in 2020, regulates businesses in areas like e-money issuance and digital payment services, thereby capturing crypto exchanges and wallets into its regulatory net.

By mapping out the regulatory framework of various jurisdictions, it's evident that navigating this complex terrain necessitates an understanding of a wide range of diverse, jurisdiction-specific regulations and legal classifications. It's essential for businesses operating in this space to remain robustly updated on regulatory developments specific to each jurisdiction where they have a significant business interest. This will offer them the advantage of ensuring compliance while harnessing the potential of this innovative technology to the maximum. Not only does this foster healthy market competition, but it also paves the way for a regulatory environment that promotes stability and mitigates potential systemic risks.

Chapter 4. Compliance in Blockchain: The Why and How

In the rapidly evolving landscape of cryptocurrencies and blockchain, compliance has become a term of significance. Essentially, it refers to how well a company or individual aligns with legal, ethical, and professional standards imposed by governing authorities. For firms and enthusiasts vested in the blockchain sphere, the concept of compliance is not a mere formality but a critical endeavor that has far-reaching implications.

4.1. The Imperative of Compliance

The vigorous growth of blockchain technology and its applications has caught the attention of regulatory authorities worldwide. Numerous federal and international agencies are actively involved in formulating regulatory policies concerning blockchain to protect consumers, prevent illegal activities, and maintain economic stability. Thus, anyone operating in the blockchain domain must understand and adhere to these regulations, or in other words, ensure compliance to prevent legal repercussions.

Compliance not only safeguards an organization from potential penalties and fines but also improves its reputation among investors, customers, and the larger community. Improved transparency and commitment to ethical standards attracts a larger user base and increases trust.

4.2. Components of Compliance

In the world of blockchain, compliance encompasses several aspects, but it primarily revolves around the following core components:

AML (Anti-Money Laundering): AML regulations are designed to prevent individuals or organizations from making income through illegal actions. In the blockchain world, these regulations help prevent transactions that involve funds obtained from illegal activities.

KYC (Know Your Customer): KYC procedures are critical in the financial world to prevent identity theft, fraud, and other illegal activities. These procedures require businesses to verify the identity of their clients and assess potential risks.

CFT (Counter Financing of Terrorism): CFT regulations are enacted to cut off the money supply to entities involved in terrorist activities. Any entity operating in blockchain should ensure that its operations or platforms are not being used to fund terrorism.

4.3. Navigating Compliance in Blockchain

Navigating compliance in the realm of blockchain can indeed appear like a Herculean task, primarily due to the regulatory maze across various jurisdictions. However, with the right approach, it's a step that profoundly aids in building a trustworthy, reliable blockchain business.

Study Regulations: Understand laws and regulations, including AML, KYC, and CFT, in your region of operation. Compliance requirements may change based on your location, so it's vital to stay updated to ensure timely compliance.

Implement Compliance Protocols: Compliance should not be a one-time affair but an on-going program. It could involve regular audits, evaluations, and risk assessments.

Educate Employees: Employees play a significant role in an organization's compliance posture. Therefore, providing necessary education and training is important to be fully compliant.

Use Compliance Tools: There are software tools available that can facilitate compliance management. They can automate compliance activities, provide real-time alerts, and maintain audit trails, making the overall compliance process seamless and efficient.

4.4. The Future of Blockchain Compliance

As blockchain evolves and becomes more mainstream, it is expected to invite more regulatory oversight. Businesses will need to adapt to these changes swiftly and nimbly. A robust compliance program will give organizations an edge over competitors by winning the trust of investors, partners, and customers.

Furthermore, we expect to see advancements in regulatory technology (RegTech) solutions that will make the process of compliance smoother and more efficient, even as the legal landscape becomes increasingly complex. Tools leveraging machine learning and AI can potentially automate much of the compliance workload.

In conclusion, navigating and adhering to the intricate labyrinth of regulations within the blockchain universe might appear bewildering at first, but it doesn't have to be an uphill battle. With the right approach and tools, it's a path that leads to trust, legitimacy, and long-term success. Compliance no longer remains a choice while dealing in this disruptive technology platform; instead, it has emerged as a linchpin of survival and growth in the amplified blockchain ecosystem.

Chapter 5. Understanding Jurisdiction-specific Laws

Blockchain regulatory landscapes differ vastly across jurisdictions, thanks to the unique political, economic, and social dynamics that shape every nation's approach to the technology. The comprehension of jurisdiction-specific laws is thus a significant step in charting an informed and legal path in the blockchain space. This chapter seeks to provide a solid foundation for understanding jurisdiction-specific laws, focusing on key regions with distinct approaches to blockchain regulation.

5.1. The United States

The United States has a multifaceted legal approach to blockchain, with various federal and state agencies exercising oversight. For instance, the Securities and Exchange Commission (SEC) tends to categorize many Initial Coin Offerings (ICOs) as securities, implying that they fall under existing securities regulations.

Concurrently, the Commodities Futures Trading Commission (CFTC) views cryptocurrencies as commodities, meaning trading of virtual currencies is subject to commodity trading laws. Furthermore, the Internal Revenue Service (IRS) classifies cryptocurrencies as property, with implications for taxes on gains and losses.

State-wise, while some states such as Arizona and Wyoming have embraced blockchain technology, others like New York have enacted stringent regulations, especially for cryptocurrency businesses.

5.2. European Union

The European Union has shown signs of in-depth understanding and adoption of blockchain technology. The EU's approach is integrated, with an aim to avoid fragmented regulations among member states. The EU Blockchain Observatory and Forum were set up to unite states and ensure the blockchain's policies harmonize across borders.

It is, however, pertinent to note that individual countries like Malta and Estonia have taken proactive steps in adopting blockchain-friendly regulations, inviting global blockchain companies to set up operations within their borders.

5.3. China

China presents a unique picture of blockchain regulation. It affords a dichotomy of an outright ban on cryptocurrency trading and ICOs, contrasted with a robust embrace of blockchain technology. The government prioritizes blockchain patents and uses the technology extensively in various public sectors - a testament to its split persona towards blockchain.

5.4. Singapore

The Monetary Authority of Singapore (MAS), similar to the U.S SEC, has chosen not to regulate the technology itself but considers the activities surrounding the technology under its purview. For instance, if digital tokens constitute capital market products under the Securities and Futures Act, the relevant laws are applicable.

5.5. The Gulf Cooperation Council (GCC)

Within GCC countries, some like Bahrain and the United Arab Emirates are becoming blockchain hubs by providing regulatory sandboxes for testing blockchain systems. Conversely, others like Saudi Arabia exhibit extreme caution towards cryptocurrencies though they appreciate the underlying blockchain technology.

5.6. Formulating Comprehensive Compliance Strategies

Acknowledging these disparities underlines the importance of tailor-fit compliance strategies for every jurisdiction a blockchain operation seeks to penetrate. Mere compliance with SEC regulations might not suffice in complying with regulations in the EU or China. Blockchain entities must seek local legal advice and understand the national regulatory framework to operate legally and effectively.

Developing a jurisdiction-specific compliance strategy begins by identifying the technology's usage and the area of law potentially applicable. For example, data privacy laws in the EU, such as the General Data Protection Regulation, may apply to a Bitcoin payment system due to the data touching EU soil.

Having grasped the concept of jurisdiction-specific laws, it is clear that the legal landscape of the blockchain is as multi-faceted and versatile as the technology itself. Understanding and aligning with these laws have never been more crucial in this era. With a careful approach, blockchain enthusiasts and businesses can seize the opportunities offered by this remarkable technology, all while squarely within the legal framework.

Chapter 6. Legality of ICOs and Tokenization : A Deep Dive

Initial coin offerings (ICOs) and Tokenization are domains within the blockchain universe that have gained significant attention, both for their innovative potential and the legal complexities they pose. Therefore, it is paramount to navigate through their legal nuances diligently. In this chapter, we will carry out an exhaustive analysis of the varied aspects that impact these blockchain functionalities and their symbiotic relationship with the complex web of legal frameworks.

6.1. Understanding Initial Coin Offerings (ICOs)

An ICO, or initial coin offering, is an often-used fundraising strategy utilized by companies within the blockchain and cryptocurrency space. However, with increasing popularity, the ICO landscape has attracted regulatory scrutiny worldwide. The reason being, token generation events that take place during an ICO can bear a striking resemblance to securities offerings. It's essential to dive deep into this resemblance to get a clear understanding of the regulatory risks.

The litmus test for determining whether an offering is a security in the U.S is known as the Howey Test, which originates from a Supreme Court case. Under this test, a transaction is a securities offering if it involves an investment of money in a common enterprise, with the expectance of profits predominantly from the efforts of others. While some ICO tokens are utility tokens intended for use within the project's ecosystem, without meeting these criteria, others could potentially be characterized as securities.

The key here is that regulatory authorities are less concerned with the name a company or project chooses to give its tokens and more focused on their functionalities and contributions.

6.2. Legal Challenges of ICOs

The unregulated nature of ICOs had made it a fertile ground for fraud and Ponzi schemes. The U.S Securities and Exchange Commission (SEC) and regulatory bodies worldwide are constantly striving to ensure investor protection.

Understanding the differences between a security token, a utility token, and a token as a commodity or currency has proven to be one of the most challenging aspects for regulators. Many platforms conducting ICOs present their tokens as utility tokens to avoid securities regulations. However, they often end up selling them like investment products.

This dichotomy led to regulatory actions against several entities conducting ICOs. A noteworthy instance is the SEC's action against Telegram, leading to a disgorgement of $1.2 billion, among the largest penalties to date.

Despite the legal complexities, clarity is emerging as regulatory agencies continue their dialogues with industry participants and begin officially commenting on and court-adjudicating some of the more prominent ICOs.

6.3. The Legality of Tokenization

Tokenization in the context of blockchain technology involves the conversion of rights to an asset into a digital token on a blockchain. Tokenization has the potential to impact various sectors ranging from real estate to intellectual property.

However, true to its disruptive nature, tokenization presents several legal challenges, such as determining the legal nature of tokens, protecting investors, ensuring transparency and accountability, preventing market abuse, and managing data security risks.

Tokens can represent different rights, so their legal status can also vary significantly. They can be categorized not only as securities but also as commodities, currencies, or entirely new classes of assets. Depending on the jurisdiction, various regulations may apply. Jurisdictions such as Switzerland and Malta have taken progressive steps in providing legal clarity to tokenization, while the U.S., on the other hand, relies on existing securities laws, applying them as per the nature of the token.

6.4. Adherence to Compliance Standards

As we navigate through the legal challenges posed by ICOs and Tokenization, compliance standards' adherence emerges as a critical factor of attention. Regulatory compliance standards differ across jurisdictions globally, thus organizations looking to launch an ICO or undertake Tokenization must remain diligent.

An organization must take into account the laws governing securities (if their tokens fall under that category), data protection norms, tax laws, and Anti-Money Laundering (AML) and Know Your Customer (KYC) regulations. It necessitates a comprehensive understanding of the applicable legal frameworks, a discourse with legal practitioners, and consultation of authoritative legal sources in the said jurisdiction.

In conclusion, while ICOs and Tokenization present promising prospects for businesses and investors alike, they also bring several regulatory complexities on the bandwidth of legal perspectives. As such, legal appraisal and compliance adherence should take precedence in their use. Ongoing legal discussions, regulatory developments, and ICOs court cases and their outcomes will undoubtedly continue to impact the blockchain platform legality, which, in turn, shall sternly guide their future. As blockchain technology continues to disrupt traditional business models, legal boundaries walk the tightrope, balancing the innovation drive with investor protection and diligence.

Chapter 7. Smart Contracts: Legalities and Challenges

Smart contracts have mandated a paradigm shift in the way agreements are drafted and executed. Pioneering this digital revolution are blockchain-based solutions, with their hallmark transparency, immutability, and security features. However, despite these highly promising facets, smart contracts present certain legal intricacies and practical challenges that beg comprehensive analysis and interpretation.

7.1. Understanding Smart Contracts

Smart contracts are self-executing contracts with the terms of the agreement directly written into lines of code. The "smart" component of these contracts implies that they can execute and enforce themselves without the need for third-party mediation.

Smart contracts are coded agreements embedded on a blockchain platform ensuring that all stakeholders have an immutable copy. Once the predefined conditions in the smart contract are met, the contract is automatically executed, eliminating the need for manual intervention and bypassing traditional contract execution bottlenecks.

7.2. Legal Recognition of Smart Contracts

Globally, the legal recognition of smart contracts varies greatly. While some jurisdictions acknowledge smart contracts as legally binding, others have not explicitly legislated on the matter, leading to an ambiguous legal status.

Countries like Arizona and Nevada in the United States have explicitly passed laws recognizing smart contracts. They provide that smart contracts and blockchain entries will be considered electronic records, and hence, receive legal recognition similar to traditional contracts.

However, these legislations are few and far between, and the absence of clear regulations in many other jurisdictions cloud the legal status of smart contracts. This uncertainty often poses a hurdle to widespread adoption of the technology.

7.3. The Challenge of Jurisdiction and Applicable Law

One of the staples of any contract is the understanding of jurisdiction and the applicable law. In the world of smart contracts, this becomes a significant hurdle.

Given the decentralized nature of blockchain, identifying a jurisdiction or applicable law can be challenging. Parties might be operating from different countries, and the servers hosting blockchain nodes could be located in multiple geographical locations. In the case of a dispute, identifying the governing law and jurisdiction could become a nightmarish ordeal.

7.4. Smart Contracts and Contract Law Essentials

Traditional contract laws demand certain conditions to be met for a contract to be legally recognized. These include offer and acceptance, capacity to contract, lawful subject matter, consideration, and mutual consent. How these principles translate into the domain of smart contracts presents complications.

Without an explicit act of offer and acceptance, it is a challenge to establish the existence of a smart contract in legal terms. Also, the typical click-wrap or browse-wrap agreements used in digital formats may not be appropriate for blockchain interfaces, calling for the need to evolve contract formation laws for the digital age.

The anonymity inherent to blockchain technology can also complicate matters, as contract law requires identifiable parties entering into an agreement willingly. Determining capacity to contract may become a hurdle, especially considering that a contractual party could be a minor or an AI algorithm (which is not acknowledged as a legal entity in most jurisdictions).

7.5. Security Risks and Vulnerabilities

Although smart contracts are generally touted to be secure due to their association with blockchain technology, they are not totally immune from attacks. A glaring example is the DAO (Decentralized Autonomous Organization) hack in 2016, where an attacker exploited a vulnerability in Ethereum's smart contract to siphon off 3.6 million Ether.

Smart contracts, like any software, can have bugs and vulnerabilities. While the immutability of blockchain is generally considered an advantage, it becomes a double-edged sword in case of flawed smart contracts, as these contracts cannot be easily altered or nullified after deployment.

7.6. Dispute Resolution and Enforcement

In a traditional contract, when a dispute arises, parties can resort to courts or arbitration. However, in case of a smart contract, the typical route to dispute resolution is less clear.

Decentralized blockchain networks lack a centralized authority, which can complicate enforcement of a legal ruling. Moreover, the traceability and enforceability issues compounded by the pseudonymity or potential anonymity of blockchain users present unique challenges.

While decentralized dispute resolution mechanisms can be coded into a smart contract, these systems are nascent and untested in many real-world scenarios.

7.7. The Legal Void and the Way Forward

Embracing the immense potential of smart contracts must not blind stakeholders to the legal risks and challenges incumbent in their use. An urgent need is for legislative bodies to acknowledge and address these challenges.

Until the legal void is filled, it might be pragmatic to combine smart contracts with traditional legal contracts in a hybrid approach. These 'Ricardian contracts' could provide the best of both worlds, offering the automation and efficiency of smart contracts, while still being enshrining the power of legal enforceability and established dispute resolution mechanisms.

Moreover, further technological development is required to address security risks. Builders of smart contracts need to adopt coding best practices, perform rigorous testing for vulnerabilities, and ideally, integrate escape clauses or update mechanisms to correct potential errors.

Navigating this myriad of legal complexities and challenges requires a collaborative effort from legislators, technologists, legal practitioners, and blockchain stakeholders. Only then can the full potential of these digital agreements be safely and effectively realized.

Chapter 8. Decentralized Finance (DeFi): Regulatory Considerations

Decentralized Finance presents significant freedoms to the world of finance, but along with them come new regulatory requirements and considerations. It is important to approach these issues with an open mind and a robust understanding of the current regulatory landscape.

8.1. Regulatory Landscape

Decentralized Finance, or DeFi, operates on the principle of open source protocols and decentralized applications (dApps), delivering financial services without a centralized authority. Although this concept challenges traditional financial intermediaries, it also raises significant regulatory considerations.

Regulators focus primarily on protecting consumers, maintaining market integrity and mitigating systemic risks. But in the DeFi environment, where there is no central party to regulate, they face challenges in applying traditional mechanisms. Even determining jurisdiction can be problematic, as blockchain networks are not confined by national borders.

As DeFi evolves, global regulatory authorities are struggling to monitor and regulate these emerging platforms. Local regulations remain inadequate due to the cross-border nature of transactions, and there's a call for a global regulation schema that could address these unique challenges.

8.2. Compliance and Risks

While the sector is still largely unregulated, some activities might fall under existing regulatory frameworks relating to securities, derivatives, and collective investment funds. For instance, if tokens issued through a DeFi protocol have characteristics of a security, the protocol could be subject to securities regulations.

Users and developers should consider the legal implications of their activities on DeFi platforms. For instance, platforms offering lending and borrowing services could be viewed as conducting banking activities, which would necessitate a banking license in many jurisdictions. Failure to comply could result in enforcement action by regulators.

Additionally, smart contracts, the backbone of DeFi platforms, face legal ambiguity. As self-executing contracts without intermediaries, their legal status is largely undefined. While they could be considered a form of contract, they may not satisfy all the legal requirements for contracts in specific jurisdictions.

8.3. Anti-Money Laundering (AML) and Know Your Customer (KYC)

AML and KYC requirements represent significant regulatory considerations for DeFi platforms. Traditional financial institutions implement thorough identity verification processes, but DeFi platforms often allow users to remain anonymous. This anonymity can potentially facilitate malicious activities, such as money laundering or other financial crimes.

Despite the decentralized nature of platforms, stakeholders could still face AML and KYC requirements. For instance, in cases where stakeholders act as money transmitters, such requirements might be applied.

Privacy coins also affect compliance. Platforms allowing privacy coin transactions could face increased scrutiny, as these transactions can be used to hide illegal activities. While privacy is a fundamental value proposition of many DeFi and blockchain solutions, it may conflict with regulatory obligations around transparency.

8.4. DeFi and Tax Implications

Investors in DeFi protocols also need to be aware of potential tax implications. Just like traditional financial investments, earning interest, capital gains and income through DeFi protocols could be subject to income tax. However, the decentralized nature of DeFi makes it difficult for tax authorities to track these transactions. In most jurisdictions, the responsibility lies with the individual to report their earnings accurately.

As the DeFi sector continues to develop and mature, it is imperative for all involved to always consider regulators' underlying objectives: protecting consumers, ensuring market integrity and mitigating systemic risk. Operating within a framework that supports these objectives could accelerate adoption and influence future legislative developments in a potentially beneficial way.

8.5. Towards a Global Regulatory Framework

Creating a global regulatory framework for DeFi appears to be the only viable solution that could help address these challenges. It requires international collaboration and dialogue to shape an environment where DeFi can grow responsibly without sacrificing user protection.

However, reaching a consensus on global blockchain regulations might be an uphill battle due to the differences in regulatory approaches among jurisdictions. It calls for innovation in regulatory technologies to effectively supervise and enforce regulations without stifling the growth of this promising sector.

The road towards regulatory clarity in the DeFi landscape seems to be long and winding. The key to promoting innovation while ensuring the safety and integrity of the financial system lies in finding a balanced approach, one that embraces the potential of DeFi while mitigating its risks. This journey will no doubt be challenging, but the rewards may well make it worth the effort. It's clear that the conversation around DeFi regulation is only just beginning – and all stakeholders have a role to play in this emerging dialogue.

Chapter 9. Navigating Privacy Laws and Data Protection

Undoubtedly, the understanding of privacy laws and data protection within the realm of the evolving blockchain world represents a complex and crucial endeavor. This knowledge is essential to ensure compliance with regional, national, and international regulations in this global digital frontier.

9.1. Understanding Privacy Laws

To satisfactorily traverse the intersection of privacy law and blockchain, you need to fathom the fundamentals of privacy law. At its core, privacy law aims to mediate the delicate balance between the individual's right to keep personal data private and the state's interest in collecting and using such data.

For instance, the European Union's General Data Protection Regulation (GDPR) and the California Consumer Privacy Act (CCPA) reflect this balance. While the GDPR is focused on protecting EU citizens' data, the CCPA aims to safeguard California residents, although their stipulations have a much broader reach due to the interconnectedness of the digital world.

It's important to realize that privacy laws differ widely by jurisdiction and sector. In some regions, privacy laws are comprehensive with strict enforcement, while in other jurisdictions, privacy policies exist in a more fragmented form or may even be absent. Consequently, a thorough knowledge of the applicable laws is imperative for any entity venturing into the blockchain universe.

9.2. Data Protection Concerns in Blockchain

Because a blockchain is inherently a distributed ledger that records transactions across multiple computers, issues concerning data protection naturally arise. As an immutable ledger, your previous transactions are securely recorded, and interference is impossible. However, this same characteristic also makes data deletion challenging, thus raising GDPR concerns.

Another concern is data dissemination. As soon as a node joins a blockchain network, it gets a copy of all the blocks present on the chain, which includes the transactions and the personal data within them. This trait of blockchain raises questions regarding data sharing and disclosure principles.

The use of pseudonyms is another aspect where the blockchain universe diverges from conventional privacy norms. Traditionally, personal data is directly linked to an individual's identity. However, in a blockchain, these transactions are linked to a pseudonym, a coded substitute for the participant's identity. While pseudonymization is a recommended measure under the GDPR, deciphering this subtle nuance can be challenging.

9.3. Adapting To Privacy Laws

Given the conflicts between the inherent characteristics of the blockchain and existing privacy laws, compliance becomes a challenging but indispensable task.

Now, let's look into some of the ways forward:

1. Geo-Fencing: Geo-fencing refers to setting up virtual boundaries, making the system respect the physical location of the users or data. Implementing geo-fencing in blockchain can ensure

regional privacy norms are adhered to.

2. GDPR-Compliant Blockchains: The development of GDPR-compliant blockchains, where user data can be modified, corrected, or deleted, appears to be a viable solution.

3. Encryption: Implementing superior levels of encryption, even for stored data, can reduce security threats.

4. Hybrid Blockchains: Private blockchains controlled by a single entity can comply with privacy laws more easily. Thus, a blended approach of private and public blockchain might be a way out.

9.4. Maintaining Robust Compliance Practices

Maintaining strong compliance practices is necessary to navigate around potential legal pitfalls associated with privacy laws and data protection in the blockchain universe.

To create a seamless compliance framework, organizations should:

1. Conduct regular Privacy Impact Assessments (PIA)

2. Understand and update their Privacy Policy considering ICO's guidance

3. Respect individuals' rights to access, rectification, erasure, and restrict processing

4. Have a justifiable lawful basis to process personal data

5. Appoint a Data Protection Officer (DPO) if necessary

6. Keep themselves updated with evolving privacy laws and data protection regulations in their respective jurisdictions

9.5. The Path Ahead

As we embark on the digital frontier's journey, privacy laws' importance in the blockchain world cannot be overstated. Acknowledging and appreciating the associated challenges and taking proactive steps to deal with them will not just ensure compliance, rather will also ensure trust and success in this fluctuating yet fascinating landscape.

Ultimately, it's this understanding of the complexities of privacy laws and a willingness to adhere to them that will guide you in your journey through the intricate maze of blockchain regulations.

Chapter 10. Risk Assessment and Management in Blockchain

Risk assessment and management play pivotal roles in any blockchain application. These twin disciplines are about understanding and responding to potential difficulties. In a blockchain landscape, these difficulties may take the form of regulatory uncertainties to technical challenges or threats coming from cybercriminals.

10.1. Identifying Potential Risks in Blockchain Applications

When you're dealing with blockchain applications, the first step in risk management is to understand common potential risks. While the inherent properties of blockchain, such as its decentralized nature and immutable record, offer significant advantages, these components also create unique risk profiles. Here are some commonplace risks:

- **Technical Risks**: Because blockchain is relatively new and continually evolving, applications might encounter unexpected bugs or vulnerabilities. Technical risks also include potential pitfalls in the software design and problematic coding practices.

- **Regulatory Risks**: Given that blockchain crosses several jurisdictions with differing regulatory environments, it can face a daunting web of complex laws and guidelines. These regulations can impact everything from ICOs (Initial Coin Offerings) to privacy concerns.

- **Operational Risks**: These include the risk associated with the operational aspects of a blockchain. For instance, potential risks could be tied to the onboarding of new participants, security of digital wallets, and execution of smart contracts.

- **Security Risks**: Despite blockchain's innate security protocols, cyber-attacks still pose a significant threat. These attacks could aim to steal cryptocurrencies in wallets, manipulate weak points in the blockchain's structure or attack exchanges and digital infrastructure.

10.2. Risk Assessment Methods

After identifying the potential risks, a comprehensive risk assessment is essential. There are multiple methods to perform risk assessment, which generally involves studying possible outcomes and their probabilities. Here are some commonly adopted methods:

- **Quantitative Risk Assessment**: This approach involves assigning numerical values to the probability and impact of risks. It's particularly useful when dealing directly with financial terms or tangible assets.

- **Qualitative Risk Assessment**: Instead of precise numerical values, this method utilizes descriptive terms to represent the probability and impact of risks. This approach is better suited for subjective or hard to measure risks.

- **Scenario Analysis**: Particularly useful for blockchain applications due to its complex and unpredictable nature. This technique involves devising potential future scenarios, then analyzing outcomes and managing them.

It's crucial to remember there isn't a 'one-size-fits-all' approach to risk management. The selection of a risk assessment method should be based on the unique dynamics of the specific blockchain application, its technical infrastructure, and its operating landscape.

10.3. Mitigation and Management of Risks

Risk mitigation involves developing strategies designed to manage and reduce the impact of identified risks. These strategies may take several forms based on the nature of the risk. Here are some widespread management principles:

- **Risk Avoidance**: This strategy involves making changes to the blockchain project's procedures, activities or components to completely avoid the risk.

- **Risk Transfer**: The blockchain project could transfer the risk to another party through contracts, insurance, or other means.

- **Risk Mitigation**: This entails reducing the impact or likelihood of the risk by implementing controls, such as using secure coding practices, setting up regular software updates, implementing security policies and controls, or improving user education and awareness.

- **Risk Acceptance**: Sometimes, it might be more cost-effective or practical for the blockchain project to accept the risk. This decision should always be consciously made rather than the result of ignorance or neglect.

While mitigation addresses each risk individually, it's crucial to devise a comprehensive risk management plan. This plan integrates the blockchain's broader logistics and systematically aligns the mitigation strategies with business objectives and regulatory prerequisites.

10.4. Risk Management Models in Blockchain

Several risk management models have been developed that can be readily applied to blockchain technologies. Two of the most famous are OCTAVE (Operationally Critical Threat, Asset, and Vulnerability Evaluation) and FAIR (Factor Analysis of Information Risk). Both models offer valuable methodologies and tools for assessing and managing blockchain risks.

The OCTAVE model is designed to help organizations identify and evaluate security risks, focusing on organizational, technological, and operational aspects. The FAIR model, meanwhile, provides a standard taxonomy and ontology for risk management. This model is particularly effective for understanding, analyzing, and quantifying information risk in financial terms to assist decision-making.

To summarize, understanding and managing risks is of paramount importance in ensuring the smooth execution of blockchain applications. An informed, forward-thinking approach to risk management can enhance a blockchain project's resilience, profitability, and long-term viability. Moreover, as the blockchain landscape evolves and matures, risk management will only grow in importance and complexity, making it an indispensable skill to master.

Chapter 11. Crypto Taxation and Anti-Money Laundering (AML) Rules

Understanding the interplay between cryptocurrency and taxation, as well as Anti-Money Laundering (AML) rules, is paramount in the new age of digital assets. This can help to circumvent potential legal consequences and penalties by ensuring your operations align with regional and international standards.

11.1. The Scope of Crypto Taxation

The tax laws of different jurisdictions around the world react differently to cryptocurrencies, each defining and classifying them in their unique way. Some countries view cryptocurrencies as a type of property, others consider them a form of money, while a few may classify them as commodities or securities.

The tax implications of these classifications represent a central challenge that potential and current digital asset holders must grapple with. Essentially, the way you report your taxes and the rate you'd pay depends on how your jurisdiction classifies cryptocurrencies. This variance emphasizes the importance of getting professional tax advice tailored for your particular circumstances and location.

Transactional data encoded on the blockchain can also be another point of interest for taxation. Given the transparent nature of most blockchain technologies, transaction details including sender, receiver, and amount can be publicly viewed, providing tax authorities with a mechanism for identifying tax evaders. A word of caution, though: misreporting or underreporting can lead to complications with regulatory bodies, so it is crucial to ensure full compliance in line with regional crypto taxation laws.

11.2. Cryptocurrency Tax Event Examples

From a general perspective, the following scenarios represent the most common taxable events related to cryptocurrency:

1. Selling cryptocurrency for fiat money, like USD or EUR

2. Trading one cryptocurrency for another cryptocurrency

3. Earning cryptocurrency as income (either as an employee or through mining/other processes)

4. Using cryptocurrency to pay for goods or services

This list isn't comprehensive, as taxation depends significantly on local jurisdictions. However, using these examples as a guide provides a decent starting point in understanding crypto taxation.

11.3. Tax Avoidance Vs Tax Evasion

The terms tax avoidance and tax evasion are commonly used in the context of taxation, so it's essential to understand the difference. Tax avoidance refers to legal means of reducing tax liability, such as using tax deductions and credits, whereas tax evasion involves illegal tactics to avoid paying taxes, like misreporting income or creating fraudulent tax documents.

Crypto taxation involves both aspects, as several jurisdictions offer legal avenues to minimize tax exposure, such as taxable losses from cryptocurrency investments. However, due to the perceived anonymous nature of certain cryptocurrencies, some attempt tax evasion, a practice that law enforcement agencies around the world are actively countering.

11.4. Anti-Money Laundering (AML) Rules

AML regulations pose another legal parameter that all cryptocurrency users must thoroughly comprehend. Broadly defined, AML rules are international standards designed to prevent individuals or organizations from disguising illegally obtained funds as legitimate income. Cryptocurrencies can be used for money laundering due to their pseudonymous nature and international reach. As a result, most jurisdictions have extended existing AML regulations to apply to cryptocurrencies.

The cornerstone of most AML rules in the context of cryptocurrencies is the 'know your customer' (KYC) process. Generally applied by exchanges and wallets, KYC process mandates these platforms verify the identity of their customers, effectively removing the anonymity associated with blockchain transactions.

Moreover, AML rules also incorporate international fund transfer instructions, where cryptocurrency service providers must submit information about the sender and receiver for transactions over a certain threshold. These regulations help global regulatory agencies to track money flows and identify suspicious activity.

11.5. Cryptocurrency Compliance and Law Enforcement

Compliance with tax laws and AML rules is not optional but a fundamental element of participating in the cryptocurrency landscape. Legislation has been rapidly evolving to keep pace with the growth of the crypto industry, and several law enforcement agencies now specialize in blockchain analysis to enforce legal compliance.

Authorities, using advanced blockchain tracing capabilities, can detect illicit activities such as tax evasion or money laundering. Non-compliance risks severe penalties, including hefty fines and potential legal repercussions.

In conclusion, professional advice must be sought to better understand and comply with the unique challenges posed by cryptocurrency taxation and AML rules. It's crucial to familiarize ourselves with the legal maze around this technology, as blindly navigating this complex landscape can lead to detriments, both financially and legally.

www.ingramcontent.com/pod-product-compliance
Lightning Source LLC
Chambersburg PA
CBHW071047260726
48661CB00007B/3184